WILDLIFE AT RISK

ENDANGERED
GIANT PANDAS

Jane Katirgis and Carl R. Green

Enslow Publishing

101 W. 23rd Street
Suite 240
New York, NY 10011
USA
enslow.com

Published in 2016 by Enslow Publishing, LLC.
101 W. 23rd Street, Suite 240, New York, NY 10011

Library of Congress Cataloging-in-Publication Data
Katirgis, Jane, author.
 Endangered giant pandas / Jane Katirgis and Carl R. Green.
    pages cm. —(Wildlife at risk)
 Summary: "Discusses giant pandas, why they are endangered, and how they are being helped"-- Provided by publisher.
 Audience: Ages 11+.
 Audience: Grades 7 to 8.
 Includes bibliographical references and index.
 ISBN 978-0-7660-6894-0 (library binding)
 ISBN 978-0-7660-6892-6 (pbk.)
 ISBN 978-0-7660-6893-3 (6-pack)
 1. Giant panda—Juvenile literature. 2. Endangered species—Juvenile literature. 3. Giant panda—Conservation—Juvenile literature. I. Green, Carl R., author. II. Title.
 QL737.C27K374 2016
 599.789—dc23
                    2015010125

Printed in the United States of America

To Our Readers: We have done our best to make sure all Web site addresses in this book were active and appropriate when we went to press. However, the author and the publisher have no control over and assume no liability for the material available on those Web sites or on any Web sites they may link to. Any comments or suggestions can be sent by e-mail to customerservice@enslow.com.

Portions of this book originally appeared in the book *The Giant Panda*.

Contents

Giant Pandas at a Glance

Scientific Name

Ailuropoda melanoleuca. The Chinese call the giant panda *da xiong mao* (dah-shong mah-oo)—the "large cat-bear."

Closest Relatives

The giant panda is most often classified as a member of *Ursidae*—the bears. As a bear, its closest relative is the South American spectacled bear. Other scientists argue that the giant panda is a member of *Procyonidae*—the raccoons. In that family, its closest relative would be the red panda.

Current Habitat

All wild giant pandas live in the dense bamboo forests of the mountains of western China.

Size and Weight*

Adult Male: Length: 4 to 6 ft. (1.2 to 1.8 m)
    Height: 27 to 32 in. (69 to 81 cm)
    Weight: 230 lbs. (104 kg)
Adult Female: Length: 3.5 to 4.5 ft.(1.1 to 1.4 m)
    Height: 24 to 30 in. (61 to 76 cm)
    Weight: 198 lbs. (89.8 kg)

Diet

Giant pandas feed on the shoots, leaves, and stems of the bamboo. In one year, an adult panda can consume more than ten thousand pounds of bamboo. On occasion, pandas also eat fish, small rodents, honey, and flowering plants.

Current Populations

Estimates place the wild population of giant pandas at about 1,600. Another 300 live in zoos and breeding centers, most of which are in China.

Special Adaptations

The giant panda uses a thumb-like wrist bone to grasp bamboo stalks. Its thick, dense coat protects it from cold, snow, and rain at altitudes as high as 10,500 feet (3,200 m).

Life Span

In the wild: about 20–22 years.
In captivity: up to 30 years.

Vocalizations

Giant pandas have a large vocabulary. They chirp during mating, honk in times of stress, and bark or click their teeth to frighten enemies. A squeal signals submission or pain, and a bleating, goat-like sound indicates a friendly contact.

Main Threats

Habitat destruction, poaching, periodic die-offs of bamboo, and loss of genetic diversity.

Legislative Status

In the United States, pandas are protected by the Endangered Species Act of 1973. Zoos that want to import pandas must follow strict rules from the Fish and Wildlife Service. China created the first of its giant panda reserves in 1963.

Organizations Working to Save the Panda

Center for Reproduction of Endangered Species

China Wildlife Conservation Association

World Wildlife Fund

Zoological Society of San Diego; Zoo Atlanta; National Zoological Park; Memphis Zoo

*Figures represent average measurements.

chapter one

MEET AILUROPODA MELANOLEUCA

Perhaps you think it is just a typical day at the zoo. Children delight in the antics of the sea lions at feeding time. Spectators watch in awe as a tiger paces around its cage. Not far away, children giggle as a kangaroo rat bounces through its home at the mammal house. In another exhibit, a giraffe stretches its endlessly long legs.

As it turns out, this is far from being a normal day. The zoo has just welcomed some new guests. Follow the surging crowd to the enclosure where *Ailuropoda melanoleuca* lives. There is the zoo's new star calmly munching a bamboo stalk. Someone whispers, "She's a real live black-and-white teddy bear!" You do not need a sign to tell you that you are face-to-face with China's best-loved visitor—the giant panda.

People Love Pandas

Why do people adore the giant panda? Scientists believe the answer lies in the panda's nonthreatening looks. Like toddlers, pandas have large heads and round, flat faces. Also like babies, their bodies give the illusion of being soft and cuddly. Even the panda's eyes look big and gentle thanks to its black eye patches.[1]

Of course, giant pandas are ten times the size of a human baby. Even so, these slow-moving bamboo eaters inspire joy, not fear. Watch a panda at play. You cannot help but smile to see it turn in clumsy somersaults. If a soccer ball is thrown into the pen, the panda will likely play a lively game—until its sharp claws rip the ball to shreds.[2]

Chinese philosophy, art, and science are all affected by the concept of yin and yang. This relates to the ideal of opposites living together in perfect harmony. The panda is considered a living example of yin and yang because it is so comfortable in its coat of black-and-white fur.

A zookeeper answers questions about the giant panda. Her listeners look upset when she confirms that the species is in danger of extinction. Unlike animals such as snail darters and crested toads, people deeply care about pandas. That fact led the World Wildlife Fund (WWF) to pick the giant panda as its symbol. Today, a black-and-white panda logo carries the WWF's conservation message across the globe.

Giant Panda Legend

There are many stories about how the panda got its patches of black fur. An old Tibetan legend tells us that pandas once were as white as polar bears. In that long-ago time, a panda cub played with a flock of sheep tended by four sisters. One day a leopard sprang at the cub. The sisters grabbed their shepherd's crooks and tried to chase the predator away. In the confusion, the cub escaped. The angry leopard turned on the girls and killed them.

All of China's giant pandas came to the funeral. As a sign of their grief, they wore black armbands. When they hugged, cried, and wiped their eyes, their tears caused the dye in the armbands to run. Each hug and pat left a black splotch on their white fur. When they saw what had happened, the pandas vowed never to wash off the black markings. Later, the pandas turned the girls' graves into a mountain with four tall peaks. The mountain still stands in Sichuan Province near the Wolong Nature Reserve. Villagers call it Siguniang—the Four Sisters Mountain.

The Panda's Family Tree

Scientists long have wondered, "Is the giant panda a bear or a raccoon?" The ancient Chinese thought the panda looked like a bear, so they called it a bear. One of their many names for the panda was zhu xiong, or the bamboo bear. When modern naturalists arrived on the scene, most agreed with the old name. It seemed logical to put the giant panda in the bear family—the *Ursidae*. Others shook their heads. The giant panda, they argued, is more like the smaller raccoon-like red panda. In their minds, giant pandas belong in the raccoon family—the *Procyonidae*.[3]

Each side gathered data to prove its case. The pro-raccoon side argued that the teeth, skulls, and forepaws of giant pandas and red pandas are very much alike in size and the way they act. Both species eat bamboo. Both have similar facial markings. The people

Fast Fact!

A panda has an enlarged wrist bone that helps it grasp all the food it has to eat—up to 84 pounds (22 kg) a day!

Although the red panda has similar facial features to that of the giant panda, they are not closely related. The giant panda is considered part of the bear family, whereas the red panda is thought to belong to the raccoon family.

who thought it was more like a bear claimed that size and shape do count. Newborn bears and newborn giant pandas are much alike. As adults, pandas have big round, bear-like bodies. Their rounded ears are shaped like those of the Asiatic black bear. A red panda, by contrast, has pointed ears.

Lab work furnished the tiebreaker. Tests showed that the giant panda's blood and genetic background are more bear-like than raccoon-like. Based on those results, textbooks assigned giant pandas to the bear family on a branch of their own. Red pandas are likewise given their own branch in the raccoon family. Fossils prove that the two pandas shared a common ancestor, but each went its own way millions of years ago. The giant panda's closest modern relative is the South American spectacled bear.[4]

This long-running debate does not interest the giant panda. These animals spend their days eating and sleeping. They do not worry, scientist Edwin Colbert wrote in 1938, about the quarrels they cause just by being themselves.[5]

chapter two

Life on a Bamboo Mountain

It is winter on a high mountain ridge in China. As snow drifts from the sky, an enormous herbivore is busy inspecting its meal. The giant panda strips away the outer layer of a stalk of bamboo and gets busy eating. After eating her fill, she sits back and gets ready for a morning nap.

Everything this female panda needs is close to her: bamboo to eat and a mate feeding nearby. Even the hollow tree that will shelter her when it is time to have her baby is steps away.[1]

Mountain Home

Six-month-old panda cubs born and raised in a zoo are quite friendly and huggable. The adults are quite a different matter. Pandas look soft and playful, but they are bear-like in shape and temper. Those sharp claws and teeth have mauled a number of unlucky or unwise zookeepers.

As bears go, giant pandas are on the small side. Females weigh in at around 200 pounds (91 kg) and measure 24 to 30 inches (61 to 76 cm) at the shoulder. Mature males are 10 to 20 percent larger, tipping the scales at 230 pounds (104 kg) or more. If a big male panda could stand fully erect, he would look a six-foot (183-cm) man in the eye.

Naturalists admire the giant panda's striking black-and-white coat. The thick, oily fur protects its owner from winter cold and summer rains. Scientists guess that the panda's coat also serves as camouflage. Seen against a rocky, snow-covered hillside, the panda nearly vanishes from view. Other scientists think the panda's distinctive black-and-white coat lets pandas spot one another.[2] The bold markings might also serve as a warning to predators.

The giant panda's life is tied tightly to bamboo. It has poor eyesight, but its keen sense of smell helps it pick out the choicest shoots and stems, called culms. Nature has equipped its forepaws with what look like thumbs for grasping the tough stems and leaves. Each "thumb" is an enlarged wrist bone covered with a fleshy pad of skin. As it feeds, the panda's strong jaws and large molars crush the tough bamboo stalks. Splinters that would choke most animals slide down its leathery and mucous-lined throat.

Bamboo makes up 99 percent of the giant panda's diet. Even so, its digestive system is a holdover from an age when they ate meat, not plants. The panda's intestine, where digestion takes place, is only five to seven times its body length. By contrast, a cow's intestine measures twenty times its body length. As a result, the panda can digest only 20 percent of the bamboo's food value. A cow retains some 60 percent of the nutrients in the grass it eats.

Giant pandas must eat massive amounts of bamboo to get enough nutrition. Adults need up to 40 pounds (18 kg) of leaves

Pandas eat sitting upright so their front paws can grasp the bamboo. Their powerful jaws and teeth allow them to bite off and chew small pieces of the tough stalks.

and culms a day. If they are feeding on fresh shoots, their day's intake doubles to around 80 pounds (36 kg).[3] Because this diet contains little fat, pandas do not hibernate. They would starve if they tried to sleep the winter away in a den.

Panda Habitat

Giant pandas once roamed the mountains of Burma (now called Myanmar), Laos, Vietnam, and China. Today, human settlement has reduced the panda's territory to a handful of wildlife reserves.

All of them can be found in the rugged mountains of western China, mainly in Sichuan Province. The upland ridges are often covered in thick clouds and pelted by heavy rains and snowstorms.

The arrow and umbrella bamboos favored by giant pandas thrive at altitudes of 5,000 to 12,000 feet (1,524 to 3,658 m). Shaded by taller trees, the fast-growing stalks cluster in thick groves. One study counted one million bamboo culms per square mile. A grove of that size can support as many as five giant pandas.[4] Thanks to their high water content, the plants also supply much of the water that pandas need.

Pandas share their misty habitat with many plants and animals. In a single reserve, naturalists counted more than four thousand species of native plants. Nine species of pheasant build their nests in the mountains of Sichuan. The region's mammals include golden monkeys, porcupines, and deer.[5] Leopards, weasels, and packs of wild dogs known as dholes prey on unguarded panda cubs. All of these predators scatter when an angry mother panda lumbers to the rescue.

Fast Fact!

Wild pandas get most of their water from bamboo. You may think of this as a dry grass, but it is actually about half water.

Quiet Giants

Giant pandas shy away from contact with other animals—even other pandas. They seem content to spend quiet days feeding and resting. Even this low level of activity requires vast amounts of bamboo. Panda expert George Schaller's studies show that a panda spends up to twelve hours a day feeding. Up at dawn, the panda stuffs its stomach full of leaves, stems, and shoots. Full at last, it rests for two to four hours. Then, hungry again, it repeats the routine. As the day drifts past, the panda takes time to groom its fur and mark nearby trees with its scent.[6]

In the spring, the giant panda's lifestyle changes abruptly. For a brief two or three weeks, females come into heat. Nearby males respond to their calls and scent marks. Naturalists believe that these strong-smelling smears give clues to their maker's sex, identity, and intentions. If the male is interested, he lets loose a chorus of moans, hoots, yips, and barks. Drawn by his calls, the female seeks him out. The two must mate during the two to five days when she can become pregnant.[7] Afterward, the female returns to her own range. In most cases, the male never sees the cub he has fathered.

The female makes her den in a hollow tree. She will carry the unborn cub for 97 to 165 days. Almost all growth takes place during the last 45 to 60 days. This delay, scientists believe, allows the cub to be born when food is most plentiful. The brief growth period produces cubs that are born blind, helpless, and nearly naked. A typical cub weighs only three or four ounces (85 to 113 g). Twin births are common, but the weaker cub almost always dies. Nursed by a loving mother, the surviving cub grows quickly.

Although young giant pandas are sometimes seen resting on tree limbs, they are usually found on the ground. For shelter, they prefer caves, hollow trees, and rock crevices.

By three weeks, it weighs a robust two pounds (.9 kg). More and more it looks like a small copy of the female.[8]

The cub stays close to its mother for up to two years. During these months, she teaches it the skills it will need as an adult. By five months, the cub is strong enough to travel by her side. As weeks and months pass, it learns to feed on the bamboo that will be its adult diet. Weaning begins, and by its first birthday, nursing gradually reduces. A year later, the female comes in heat again. She drives the cub away and begins a new mating cycle. The two-year-old now weighs a hundred pounds or more. Slowly it drifts away to find its own range. By age six, the cub will be sexually mature and ready to seek its own mate.

This two-year cycle limits the number of cubs a female can raise. At best, she will give birth to only four or five cubs during her twenty-year lifetime. Of those five, only two are likely to survive. Food shortages, poachers, disease, and habitat loss are pushing giant pandas ever closer to extinction.[9]

Fast Fact!

Panda cubs do not open their eyes until they are six to eight weeks old.

chapter three

GIANT PANDA THREATS

Chinese farmers who live near the Wolong Natural Reserve set traps for local animals, such as musk deer. They sell this animal's musk gland to people who make perfume. The poor farmers try to make money to support their families. The farmers do not mean to trap giant pandas, but sometimes they get snared in the trap accidentally.

One such farmer was Leng Zhizhong. Thirty years ago, he appeared before a judge for the common crime. After hearing from both sides, the judge read his verdict. "The sentence is two years in prison," he told the poacher.

Today's punishments are far more severe. China's courts have sentenced a number of poachers to life in prison. A few have been condemned to death. In every case, the crime was the same. Each man had killed one or more giant pandas.[1]

Natural Threats

Wildlife lovers cheer any action that protects the giant panda. There are only about 1,600 pandas remaining in the wild. The threats that have been killing off the panda are both natural and human-made.

Life in the wild has always been full of hazards. Newborn cubs left alone while their mothers are feeding are easy prey for weasels. Older cubs fall victim to leopards or packs of dholes. A panda that stops eating may be fighting a different kind of killer. Roundworms stop growth and sap their host's energy. Even when it is sick, a panda seldom acts the part. Doing so would invite attack by hungry predators.[2]

In 1983, searchers found the bodies of sixty-two giant pandas in China's Qionglai Mountains. Neither poachers nor predators were to blame. The pandas starved to death after a mass die-off of arrow bamboo. Naturalists warn that die-offs are part of bamboo's life cycle. Within a region, all the plants of a bamboo species produce flowers, go to seed, and then die at the same time. The seeds will sprout, but new plants take years to mature. Depending on the species, the time between die-offs ranges from 3 to 120 years.

In ancient times, a hungry giant panda could move to a new habitat. Today, migration is not always an option. Roads, train tracks, farms, and villages have pushed high into the mountains. Pandas hate to move in the best of times. Now wary of human-made obstacles, they give up the search for new feeding areas. One by one, the stranded pandas die of hunger as the bamboo dies off.

Threats From Humans

In addition to bamboo die-offs, there are threats posed by humans. Although there has been a deep decline in illegal panda poaching, it still occurs. But most poachers do not intentionally hunt for them. The giant panda can get caught and injured or killed in a trap set for a different animal.

China passed a tough wildlife protection law in 1989. The law forbids the capture, killing, or trading of any protected species. Stiffer penalties and improved policing help, but they have not put a stop to poaching. In 1990, a WWF agent proved that fact by posing as a buyer from Taiwan. As she toured China, a dealer tried to sell her two live cubs for $112,000. At other stops, she found sixteen panda pelts for sale.[3]

Tree cutting is the primary risk to the giant panda. Once the trees are cut, bamboo stops growing and rain erodes the soil. Logging is forbidden in China's reserves, but villagers believe the forests are there to use. Firewood is costly, and many villagers are too poor to buy it. Friendly guards sometimes look the other way when they see trees being cut. In a few cases, armed woodcutters have opened fire when guards did try to stop them.[4]

Logging and loss of habitat remain the largest threats to the giant panda.

Tourists who come to see wild pandas add another type of stress. The visitors create jobs in remote areas, but the cost is high. City folk demand smooth roads, soft beds, and extra helpings of Wolong's famous smoked pork. Caring for their needs often pollutes the woods and streams. If well managed, the dollars spent by tourists can help pay for conservation measures. When tourism surges out of control, however, wildlife is the big loser.[5]

Loss of Habitat

The story dates back to an age when humans first learned the art of farming. Early farmers planted in the fertile plains and valleys. Later, with ever more mouths to feed, they pushed into the uplands. Along the way, they cut trees for fuel and lumber and hunted animals for meat and fur. Their herds overgrazed the hillsides. With forest cover lost, rain washed away the topsoil.[6]

William Sheldon saw the results when he toured China in the 1930s. "Even at two thousand feet above the river bottom," he wrote, " . . . every possible acre of earth seemed planted with corn." As he pushed higher, Sheldon saw that entire hillsides were without trees. The sight, he noted, "has been very depressing."[7] As farming advanced, the giant pandas retreated. By Sheldon's day, the bamboo bears were confined to the mountains of western China.

Today, China must feed, clothe, and house more than 1.35 billion people. Despite increasing population pressures, the government is doing its best to safeguard wild habitat. The losses, however, continue to mount. Between the mid-1970s and the mid-1980s, the panda lost 50 percent of its remaining habitat. Demand for cheap products made in China causes the country to use up more of its natural resources. If knit together, Wolong and the other reserves would cover only 5,021 square miles (13,004 km²). North America's Greater Yellowstone Ecosystem is four times that size.[8]

The plight of the 500,000-acre (202 hectares) Wolong reserve spotlights the problem. Satellite photos made in the early 1970s show the area losing 52 acres (21 hectares) of wildlife habitat per year. After the park was created in 1975, panda habitat vanished at four times that rate—237 acres (96 hectares) per year. Wolong's panda population is dropping almost as quickly. Naturalists counted 145 giant pandas there in 1974. In 1986, the count dipped to 72. By 2015, the number had increased to more than 150.

As more habitat is nibbled away, giant panda populations become more separated from each other. Small populations become inbred and lose genetic diversity. This results in lower fertility and more stillborn cubs. Should the climate change, the

Fast Fact!

Although giant pandas look cute, they are as dangerous as any other bear.

survivors will find it harder to adapt. Today, only three reserves support enough pandas to keep inbreeding from becoming a threat. In reserves with as few as twenty pandas, the problem already exists.

Villagers who share the giant panda's habitat mean no harm to their furry neighbors. Saving wildlife, however, takes a backseat when children are cold and hungry. Writer Vaclav Smil spoke to a peasant farmer who argued that the land is there to be used. "If there's a mountain, we'll cover it with wheat," the man said. "If there's water to be found, we'll use it all to plant rice."[9]

The challenge is clear. If the world wants to save the giant panda, there is work to be done.

chapter four
SAVING GIANT PANDAS

Although most people today have certainly heard of the giant panda, this was not always the case. Ancient Chinese rulers honored these creatures, but they were unknown to the rest of the world until 1869, when a missionary sent the first panda skins back to Europe. He described the giant panda as the prettiest kind of animal he knew.[1]

As word of the white bear spread, big-game hunters took up the chase. Each wanted to be the first westerner to kill a giant panda. Theodore Roosevelt Jr. and his brother Kermit were the first. In 1929, they journeyed to China in pursuit of the giant panda. Like their president father, they saw hunting as a grand sport. In the western mountains, guides led them to a panda sleeping in a tree. Both men fired, and the hapless panda fell at their feet.

In 1936, Ruth Harkness set out to complete her late husband's quest. His dream had been to capture a live cub. The trip led the American fashion designer deep into China's bamboo forests. After guides frightened away a mother panda, Harkness pulled a three-pound (1.4 kg) cub from its den. She nursed it from a bottle and named it Su-Lin. Back in the United States, "panda-monium" broke out.[2] Chicago's Brookfield Zoo soon bought Su-Lin. The zoo had its biggest influx of visitors the day the panda went on display.

Starting to Take Action

After World War II, naturalists trekked to China to study the giant panda. As they learned more about the species, a hard truth surfaced. Loss of habitat was putting the panda at risk. If the world did not act, the panda would be lost.

Governments joined hands in the 1970s to protect endangered wildlife. In the United States, Congress passed the 1973 Endangered Species Act. That same year, more than one hundred nations signed the Convention on International Trade in Endangered Species (CITES). The goal was to end the trade in rare animals and animal parts.

By the 1990s, the numbers showed that the drive to save the panda was falling short. China, with backing by the WWF, the United States, and other nations adopted a Panda Management Plan.[3] The plan lists six main goals:

- Construct more nature reserves with giant panda habitats.
- Establish safe areas between panda populations for pandas to travel between.
- Reduce poaching by doing a better job of guarding the reserves.

- Improve the rural way of life. When their lives get better, villagers are less likely to plunder the reserves for food, furs, and fuel.

- Strengthen efforts to train villagers in the need to protect the environment.

- Use captive breeding programs to find ways to improve the birth rate of wild pandas. Captive breeding programs focus on efforts to increase the number of live births of captive members of an endangered species.

Captive Breeding

Naturalists prefer to leave endangered animals free to live and breed in the wild. Giant pandas are an exception. At the best of times, a female raises only a few cubs during her lifetime. Today, with so few pandas left, wild pandas are hard-pressed to maintain their numbers. The answer may lie in captive breeding programs.

Fast Fact!

How do scientists count pandas in the wild? Volunteers hike the steep mountains looking for signs of the panda. One important sign is poop! They sift it and pick out pieces of bamboo that were not digested. Then they look at the unique bite marks, which are as unique as fingerprints to identify different pandas.

Zoos offer the giant panda protection, as well as entertainment. These young giant pandas are playing in the Shanghai Zoo in China.

Some captive animals, such as the Bengal tiger, mate readily. The giant panda is not one of them. Only through trial and error have scientists found ways to increase the panda birthrate. The first success came in 1963 with the birth of a cub at the Beijing Zoo. The first live birth outside of China came at Mexico City's Chapultepec Zoo in 1980. Since then, Mexico's pandas have produced seven more cubs. Five lived to become adults. This success rate is a far cry from the days when most zoo-born cubs died.

Don Lindburg, former leader of the giant panda team at the San Diego Zoo, praised the Wolong breeding program. "There have been two spectacular results," Lindburg says. "First, the pregnancy rate is up—way up! Second, infant survival has [greatly] improved." He credits the change to better feeding, health care, housing, and improved handling of cubs. Even at Wolong, females who give birth to twins often abandon one of them. Thanks to better formulas and bottles, the center's nursemaids are saving those cubs. Cub survival has gone from 30 percent to 90 percent since the Wolong Panda Center opened in 1980.[4]

All too often, captive males show little interest in mating. Doctors have tackled this problem by using artificial insemination. When the female is ready to conceive, they put her to sleep. Then they implant sperm drawn from a healthy male. The first success using this technique came at the Beijing Zoo in 1978. The process also allows breeders to improve genetic diversity. In 1982, sperm taken from a male in London was flown to Spain. There, it was used to conceive a healthy cub. Scientists now are looking ahead to the day when they welcome the first test tube cub into the world.

This baby panda was born at the Wolong Nature Reserve. The Reserve cares for pandas in the mountains of China's Sichuan Province. Naturalists work there to save the giant panda through research into panda breeding and bamboo ecology.

Fast Fact!

When China loaned giant pandas to zoos in America and Japan in the 1970s, it was one of the first cultural exchanges between China and the West. This exchange has been called panda diplomacy.

Wolong Nature Reserve

Wolong Nature Reserve is one of the keys to the giant panda's future. To reach the reserve, visitors follow bumpy dirt roads that climb into the Qionglai Mountains. China's crowded cities fall behind. Viewing Wolong for the first time, one visitor was awestruck. He said, "Traveling to China was a fantastic and awe inspiring adventure."[5]

Wolong meets all of the giant pandas' needs. Seven types of bamboo grow on quiet hillsides. Clear streams flow past groves of tall trees. Guards patrol the reserve to enforce the five nos. The local farmers know this to mean: no fire, no cutting trees, no hunting, no plowing, and no damaging forest regrowth.[6] With help from the WWF, the breeding center has been upgraded. The pandas kept there for study and breeding live in roomy enclosures. Pandas destined for release move to larger pens that duplicate Wolong's wild habitat.

Two cubs climb a tree in the Wolong Nature Reserve.

Much time, money, and love have flowed into the Wolong project. Even so, storm clouds hover over the reserve. The human population continues to increase, which leads to more land being cleared. Deep in the forest, more snares are being set. As settlements edge higher into the hills, pandas retreat farther up the mountain.

chapter five

THE FUTURE FOR GIANT PANDAS

Scientists believe the giant panda has a small chance to escape extinction. Without protection from poaching and with the loss of more of their mountain homes and food source, the future of the giant panda is a concern for all conservationists. Giant panda lovers are working tirelessly to save this endangered animal.

The effort takes many forms. Deep in the mountains of Sichuan, out-of-work loggers restore the habitat by planting trees on bare hillsides. At breeding centers, volunteers coax an orphan cub to eat. Schoolkids in Kansas surf the Web to watch a panda-cam broadcast from the Smithsonian National Zoo in Washington, D.C. In China, doctors restore a captive female's sight by removing a cataract.

When disaster strikes a panda reserve, people rally to help. The bamboo die-off of the early 1980s was one such event. Children around the globe lined up to give to Pennies for Pandas. Japan gave nearly $250,000 for rescue teams. Scientists stepped forward to supply aid and advice.[1]

The panda-cam at the National Zoo allows people from all over the world to catch a glimpse of these endangered animals.

Once in a while, the drive to save the giant panda grabs headlines. In Hong Kong, action superstar Jackie Chan led the cheers at Panda Day 2000. After a choir sang a tribute to the panda, Chan stepped forward. "The giant panda is our national treasure," he told his fans. "Everyone in Hong Kong should have a share in conserving giant pandas and their habitat."[2] In 2009, Chan donated more than $100,000 to adopt two pandas. He named them Cheng Cheng and Long Long.

Rent-a-Panda

The save-the-panda movement began when Su-Lin won the public's heart in the 1930s. Ever since, zoo directors have begged China to supply them with giant pandas. Zoos want pandas because they draw big crowds. Those pleas led to what some call the Rent-a-Panda program. When Los Angeles played host to the 1984 Olympics, China loaned two pandas to the local zoo. Over the next four years, loaner pandas showed up in a dozen of the world's cities.[3]

Rent-a-Panda was a moneymaker. The zoos drew overflow crowds—an increase of 750,000 paying visitors in Toronto alone. The cities enjoyed a rush of tourism, and China earned large rental fees. Called donations for conservation, these fees average hundreds of thousands of dollars per panda. China also received a chunk of the income from souvenir sales. Sponsors downplayed the money angle. Panda loans, they argued, put a spotlight on the plight of all endangered species.[4]

Jackie Chan told his fans, "The giant panda is our national treasure." The action-movie superstar adopted two giant pandas and works to spread the word about the endangered animal's need for protection.

In 2013, it cost a million dollars per year for a zoo to keep a giant panda. The typical contract was for ten years. Just a few zoos in the United States still have giant pandas.[5]

What's Next?

Millions of dollars have been raised for panda conservation, and more is needed. According to the American Zoo and Aquarium Association:

> Beyond the interests of zoos and other conservation entities is the larger issue of public concern and support. No one questions the endearing qualities of the giant panda, but unless public interest is linked to the urgent need to secure the future survival of both captive and wild populations, this enchantment will have served little more than an entertainment function.[6]

Money is being raised. In 2011, for example, David M. Rubenstein, founder of The Carlyle Group, gave the Smithsonian National Zoo's panda program a check for $4.5 million. The money will be used to run the panda program for five more years.[7] Many smaller donations have added to the total. The zoo, for example,

Fast Fact!

When a panda is born in captivity, it is hard to tell right away whether it is a boy or a girl. Instead of waiting several months, scientists do a DNA test.

invites panda lovers to "adopt" its two pandas. In return for their gift, donors receive a bundle of photos and pamphlets. Panda eco-tours, as well as adoptions, are available.

China has tried to move farmers out of the Wolong reserve with little success. To resettle one village, officials built new homes farther down the mountain. The stubborn farmers refused to move. The new farmland, they said, was not fertile enough. One man came closer to explaining the real reason. "We were born here, and we're staying here," he said. Another man added, "We don't see why we should move for some animals."[8] Since then, a plan has been hatched to send more village teenagers to college. After they graduate, planners expect them to find good jobs in the cities. The pressure on the reserve will ease as the village's population dwindles.[9]

Earthquake and Continued Work Ahead

In May 2008, a devastating earthquake struck the area. The epicenter was only miles from the Wolong Panda Center, where sixty-seven pandas were housed. Sadly, two pandas died, one is still missing, and the center was destroyed. The surviving pandas

In 2012, a giant panda is returned to its home in the China Giant Panda Protection and Research Center Base. The center had to be reconstructed after being damaged in the 2008 Sichuan earthquake.

were moved to a new location. Some were pregnant at the time of the disaster, and they went on to deliver healthy cubs.

The Wolong Panda Center is currently being rebuilt. The surrounding Nature Reserve was hit hard; 80 percent of the preserve was impacted in some way by the earthquake, and mudslides covered much of the bamboo.[10] Replanting the bamboo is a top priority for conservationists as they continue strive for the giant panda's safe future.

A Look to the Future

The road ahead is uncertain. Sometimes one step forward is followed by one step back. But breeding experts are keeping more captive-bred cubs alive, and that is good news. The wild population has also increased. Money is being raised, but more is needed. China's national government, along with the rest of the world, is committed to the task of saving the panda.

CHAPTER NOTES

Chapter 1. Meet *Ailuropoda melanoleuca*

1.   Susan Lumpkin and John Seidensticker, *Smithsonian Book of Giant Pandas* (Washington, D.C.: Smithsonian Institution Press, 2002), pp. 16–17.

2.   Judith Janda Presnall, *The Giant Panda* (San Diego, Calif.: Lucent Books, 1998), p. 54.

3.   George Schaller, *The Last Panda* (Chicago University of Chicago Press, 1993), p. 261.

4.   "Panda Facts," *Wanglang Nature Reserve*, January 22, 2001, <http://www.slack.net/~rd/wanglang/panda_facts.htm> (January 29, 2015).

5.   Quoted in Schaller, p. 267.

Chapter 2. Life on a Bamboo Mountain

1.   George Schaller, *The Last Panda* (Chicago: University of Chicago Press, 1993), p. 1.

2. "Panda Facts," *Wanglang Nature Reserve*, January 22, 2001, <http://www.slack.net/~rd/wanglang/panda_facts.htm> (January 29, 2015).

3.   Susan Lumpkin and John Seidensticker, *Smithsonian Book of Giant Pandas* (Washington, D.C.: Smithsonian Institution Press, 2002), pp. 64–68.

4.   Ibid., p. 75.

5.   Chris Catton, *Pandas* (New York: Facts on File Publications, 1990), p. 28.

6.   "Panda Facts," *Wanglang Nature Reserve*.

7.   Schaller, pp. 65–66.

8.   Ibid., pp. 82–83.

9.   Presnall, pp. 21–22.

Chapter 3. Giant Panda Threats

1. George Schaller, *The Last Panda* (Chicago: University of Chicago Press, 1993), pp. 126129.

2. Barbara Radcliffe Rogers, *Giant Pandas* (New York: Mallard Press, 1990), pp. 74, 106.

3. Schaller, p. 227.

4. Chris Catton, *Pandas* (New York: Facts on File Publications, 1990), p. 118.

5. Ibid.

6. Ibid., p. 109.

7. Rogers, p. 30.

8. Susan Lumpkin and John Seidensticker, *Smithsonian Book of Giant Pandas* (Washington, D.C.: Smithsonian Institution Press, 2002), pp. 6–7.

9. Schaller, p. 151.

Chapter 4. Saving Giant Pandas

1. Chris Catton, *Pandas* (New York: Facts on File Publications, 1990), pp. 7–8.

2. Public Broadcasting Service, "The Panda Baby," *Nature,* n.d., September 21, 2001.

3. World Wildlife Fund, "History of the Giant Panda," June 8, 2004, <http://wwf.panda.org/?13588/History-of-the-Giant-Panda> (January 29, 2015).

4. Pandas International, *Hetaoping Wolong Panda Center,* n.d., <http://www.pandasinternational.org/wptemp/panda-reserves/old-wolong-panda-center> (January 29, 2015).

5. San Diego Zoo, "World Wide Tours," 2014, <http://www.sandiegozoo.org/travel/testimonials.html > (January 29, 2015).

6. George Schaller, *The Last Panda* (Chicago: University of Chicago Press, 1993), p. 228.

Chapter 5. The Future for Giant Pandas

1. Chris Catton, *Pandas* (New York: Facts on File Publications, 1990), p. 77.

2. "Panda Day 2000," *Hong Kong Society for Panda Conservation,* n.d., <http://www.hkpanda.org/public_pandaday.htm> July 22, 2002.

3. Audra Ang, "Critics Question China's Worldwide Panda Profit," The Age, April 5, 2003, < http://www.theage.com.au/articles/2003/04/04/1048962931531.html > (January 29, 2015).

4. Ibid.

5. Giant Panda Zoo, *Pandas in the United States of America,* n.d., <http://www.giantpandazoo.com/panda/history/pandas-in-the-united-states-of-america> (January 29, 2015).

6. Dr. Donald G. Lindburg, coordinator, "Giant Panda," *American Zoo and Aquarium Association,* 2002, <http://www.giantpandaonline.org> (September 5, 2003).

7. Reuters, "Big Donation for Giant Panda Program at the National Zoo," *New York Times,* December 19, 2011, <http://www.nytimes.com/2011/12/20/us/big-donation-for-giant-panda-program-at-national-zoo.html?_r=0> (January 29, 2015).

8. Presnall, pp. 74–75.

9. "Panda-Friendly Forests Disappearing," April 6, 2002, <http://wc.arizona.edu/papers/94/131/01_97_m.html > (January 29, 2015).

10. Pandas International, *2008 Earthquake,* n.d. <http://www.pandasinternational.org/wptemp/2008-earthquake> (January 29, 2015).

Glossary

bamboo—A woody grass that is a large part of the giant panda's diet.

breeding program—A plan used to reproduce animals for a few generations. The program is often used by conservationists to reproduce species that are endangered.

camouflage—A way of hiding.

captive—Being confined or held in a safe place.

conservation—The protection of plants, animals, and natural resources.

culm—A stem of a certain type of grass.

endangered—In danger of becoming extinct and not existing on earth anymore

extinction—The death of an entire group, or species, of living things.

migration—The movement of a large group of animals from one place to another.

poacher—A person who kills or steals wild animals illegally.

population—The total number of people, animals, or plants living in a specific area.

predator—An animal that hunts and eats other animals for food.

roundworms—A small worm that lives inside people and animals.

species—A group of animals or plants that have similar features. They can produce offspring of the same kind.

threatened—A group of animals that is close to becoming endangered.

weaning—To transition a young animal to eating something other than its mother's milk.

Further Reading

Books

Buller, Laura. *The Great Panda Tale*. New York: DK Publishing, 2014.

Claus, Matteson. *Animals and Deforestation*. New York: Gareth Stevens Publishing, 2014.

Dudly, Karen. *Giant Pandas*. New York: Wiegl, 2013.

Murray, Julie. *Giant Pandas*. Minneapolis, Minn.: ABDO, 2013.

O'Connor, Karen. *Animals on the Verge of Extinction*. New York: Gareth Stevens Publishing, 2014.

Osborne, Mary Pope, and Natalie Pope Boyce. *Pandas and Other Endangered Species*. New York: Random House, 2012.

Yolen, Jane. Animal Stories: *Heartwarming True Tales from the Animal Kingdom*. Washington, D.C.: National Geographic Children's Books, 2014.

Web Sites

fws.gov/international/animals/giant-pandas.htm

US Fish and Wildlife Service's information about giant pandas.

pandasinternational.org/wptemp/program-areas-2/captive-breeding-program/

Learn more about the captive breeding program for giant pandas.

worldwildlife.org/species/giant-panda

Wealth of information on endangered and threatened animals.

INDEX